CORNERLESS PEOPLE

John Hartley Williams was born in Cheshire and grew up in North London. He was educated at William Ellis School, and at the universities of Nottingham and London. He now teaches English at the Free University of Berlin, where he has been since 1976. He has also lived and worked in France, Francophone Africa, Yugoslavia, and 'once spent an abominable year in Bristol, England'.

His first book, *Hidden Identities*, was published by Chatto in 1982. He won the £5000 first prize in the Arvon International Poetry Competition in 1983 with 'Ephraim Destiny's Perfectly Utter Darkness', the centrepieceof his maverick second collection *Bright River Yonder*, a baroque Wild West poetry adventure published by Bloodaxe Books in 1987 (and a Poetry Book Society Recommendation). *Cornerless People* (Bloodaxe Books, 1990) is his third book of poems.

He has organised poetry readings by visiting poets in Berlin, has promoted poetry workshops there, and was chief perpetrator of the *Gedichte mit Schärfe* Bloodaxe Berlin poetry festival in 1989. He is currently editing an anthology of contemporary British poetry for use in German schools.

JOHN HARTLEY WILLIAMS

CORNERLESS PEOPLE

BLOODAXE BOOKS

ISBN: 1 85224 101 2

First published 1990 by
Bloodaxe Books Ltd,
P.O. Box 1SN,
Newcastle upon Tyne NE99 1SN.

Bloodaxe Books Ltd acknowledges
the financial assistance of Northern Arts.

ACKNOWLEDGEMENTS

Acknowledgements are due to the editors of the following
publications in which some of these poems first appeared:
Hard Times (Berlin), *The Literary Review, Poetry Book Society
Anthology 1988-89* (PBS/Hutchinson, 1988), *Poetry Review,
The Rialto* and *Thames Poetry*. Particular thanks are due to
Christine Pagnoulle for translations of five of these poems
into French, in a bilingual section in *Pi Poëzie: Trimestrieel
Tijdschrift Voor Poëzie* (Juli-Augustus 1989).

Typesetting by Bryan Williamson, Darwen, Lancashire.

Printed in Great Britain by
Billing & Sons Limited, Worcester.

Contents

Mankind owns four things
that are no good at sea:
rudder, anchor, oars,
& the fear of going down.

ANTONIO MACHADO

… the unhappy sense of a consuming fire inside me that
was not allowed to break out, made up a sentence –
'Little friend, pour forth' – incessantly sang it to a special
tune, & squeezed & released a handkerchief in my pocket
as if it were a bagpipe.

FRANZ KAFKA

Only the underworld retains its exuberance.

GEORGES BATAILLE

Looking for You

Sometimes when I think of you
I am like a man looking for somewhere on a map.

You are there, this is where.
I keep glancing at the opened cityplan on the seat beside me

Which no red light offers pause enough
To study properly.

As usually occurs when you keep going
Hoping for the co-ordinates to co-happen, they don't.

Yr face is stern & youthful in the mirror.
There are hard blue shadows beneath yr eyes.

Why should it be necessary at all
To have to look up where you are

As if secrets would always eventually be on paper?
Is this just an excuse for the direction

We fail to take? I am still cruising the outer
Suburbs, seeking the well known mega-bargain store,

Our destination. The sky is like a piece of
Blotting paper someone has used to mop

The ink I've spilt. We're scaring up for a storm.
Truly, this is a low class district.

There are sluts in short skirts, with open bodices,
Men covered from eyelid to ankle in hair, abandoned

Bodies in prams. On that corner, people rise up & em-
Brace. They em - brace. Surely *our* street

Cannot be far away? Brick
Must have a hole in it somewhere?

Then the billboards announce
Yr colourful countenance: like Socrates' typical

Housewife, brandishing the product
Of complicity we all know & love

As wisdom. It's worth abandoning the car to climb up
And peer over...

I thought so. There it is with flags flying. Happy
Children with supermarket trolleys, & a girl that could be you,

                                        waving.

The Nurse

Under my white starched apron,
my blue coiffed hat, my black
stockings & sensible shoes
I am as naked & open as the salt sea.

Nurse Felsted, they say,
this cancer is at my throat.
Nurse Felsted, my heart
has gathered all of me into one tight fist.

I go from bed to bed
attending with uncluttered motion.
Nurse Felsted, O Christ! Nurse!
the final reproof is at my brain.

They look at me
seeing only, or partly only, or only fading
my blue coiffed hat, my black
stockings & sensible shoes

but underneath
I am as naked & open as the salt sea.

Biography

1

he certainly lived thru the
                          great events of our time:
a Jehovah's Witness knocking at the door,
                          another person, by mistake,
the garden looking wet in winter,
                          two letters

from an
old friend
not posted before he left for Australia, & never found

he was there when the car failed to start
                          one morning,
& the queen on television raised a derisive hand,
                          (a signal to someone, perhaps, who knows?)
he was outside on the vegetable patch   digging a hole
when a group
formed in the square
asking passionately 'why?'   & then went home for tea

once he forgot his own telephone number,
                          even worse,
unable to remember his own house
                          he entered another, by mistake,
noticed the resemblances
(tho they did not in the least look like one another)

& was aggrieved to find
that what had so definitely been there before

was still
not

2

he was married later
& the bride-to-be was inspected by
                          his disfigured father

to see if she was suitable to take him

                                 away from there

& would she
clip his paws
bring home the knife, if he lay oinking in the hall?

he was married in white, & the priest inquired
if it was sure he was a big enough step for the occasion
    /   he looked at the vaulting roof of the Wurlitzer
                                      & a bird flew out
& shit over the register
& shit over his wife's mother, two aunts, & a recording angel

so that when the ring came to be snapped
                              on his nose
he had already committed the crimes
                      for which this was the large arrest
& his just deserts were to see in his wife's eyes
                              a jealous lust

he trembled for
the wedding-night-to-be

for how long it would take him
to become a similar beast

3

he applied for one of life's situations
                            & went to be overlooked
in one of life's buildings   /   a porter showed
                              him the ascending cage
he went *wooshing* up to a green corridor of,
                      frankly, many exits,
the hands damp in the
toilet, liverish eyes,
& entered a room of life's extremely serious folk

who were, in all frankness, serious as life itself
as if they knew that life was serious, their own
                          careful department
quite capable of laughing now & then
                      to show how deeply unfunny things were

11

he had a desire to
burst out grinning
split seams to let them see   O

                        meritorious stuffing

but they asked him questions
beautiful, serious, sober, well-carpeted questions

& he, not finding the answer to which
gazed out of the window at the rain,

or whatever it is looks out from this

that also looks in

4 *but what was he really like?*

lent the rich money
lent the poor groans
returned his empties full
made nice young bones

mistook places for faces
wormed his way out of wealth
took mountains to molehills
kept frogs, croaked himself

went that way to go this way
came back the same
stayed put to get out of staying put
preached wine & drank blame

sold ideas by the bucket
went down the well for more
when everyone started clanking
made a dry run for the door

got there, cogitated
a splendid view of the sea
lifted his thoughts' hind-leg
at each unimaginable tree

12

warm happiness run down!
wet aftermath sting!
limped by in the sunlight
heard people chattering

had a word, anyway
had a look in the ear
of language, put a
torch up there

saw barricades of wax
a purring mob on the street
sighed & went home:
that revolutionary feat

Sicilian Hotel

Enumerating the mugs from which, one
chipped, I had drunk
innumerable teas, I saw I had taken
a number of notions out of their proper places,
                                        my own house,
its carpets, bricks,
simplicity of structure
                        had all fallen away

     Did not Arethusa turn into
     a lake,
     & Alpheus into a stream
     that he might
     continually flow into her?

At this point I made notation
of the dishes of the hotel, deep soup-cups,
a tureen, a sauce-boat

of how I had seen
the boulder Cyclops hurled at
Odysseus, it
stuck from the sea at *Aci Reale*

& I had seen his cave
near the 9th century
church
San Pietro e Paulo
which stands
thin as a Norman's brain
atop the valley

     From the balcony,
     silence . Now this is
     quietness . 2 maidens, seen
     from afar, walk bare-
     footed thru
     the inaudible surf

At bay's edge
        a pin-dark tower
unpicks the sealed sound

    Distinctive:
    these knives & forks for Apollo,
    the cheap steel of fabrication
    not silver like the sea
             which is always with us, making
    clandestine entries
             at cave-mouth...

    her tongue is fire-salamander,
             slaked on salt;
    breasts tiny & hot;
    her waist of narrows
    darkens the water into stillness

        & boys cry
        beyond the window, who
        ride their bikes against
        the traffic, one wheel

             off the ground...

My own decanters
are of plain glass, their
industrial shape
somewhat commonplace

    our waiter flickers
    (creating manners with his style)

    clears away

these plates,
superposed,
green & white napkins, crumpled...
used fish-tritons
(for grilled sardines)
Apollo's hardware

    sullied
    on cutlet

'*Ecco!*
      Take
this apple

& peel
into a bracelet for her

I have brought thee
electric wines

shocking meat, a crown
of herbs…Thy

house is far
away tonight

parola d'honore!'

Chez Marcel

When I think now
how we left there

    & the place did not change

Marcel plying us
with leery jokes,
the pinball machine...

If I had died then, playing "flipper",
local but
disputed champion, it
would have been
for limited excellence
not love

The woman was clearly in shreds.
He was deserting her

      – that French thing –

    & a whole line of parked cars
    began to move slowly, shunted
    by the rearmost, scrabbling
    for a grip on kerbside

If you could stand it
the whole winter was like that

      Other people's love-affairs.
      Other people's cars.

Pilgrims

Pilgrim explorers,
spinning
from pubs, bars,
into the street,
bidding goodbye
they climb
hands deep
in the trench of self
& plough against the wind
in any town
as lost to smoke & darkness

> *Blessed are ye*
> *that are cast out*
> *hated of men*
> *separated from company*

Fangs of drink at their brain,
gull-words like girls of night.
The last bus goes down,
None comes up, bearing
a little warmth, reproach,
aloft.
    They turn,
neither proud nor humble,
& walk
further upward
into time

Detective Story

'I have an ache in the dark,' he said,
'It forfeits delight & pleasure's misrule.
I'm a lover kicked from honesty's bed:
Look how I sleep here, alone with her jewels.'
And then he looked at me.
'I want you to find Truth,' he said.
'Go out & get her, & bring her home.'

I went into The Square, & down The Strand.
Two male clerks were kissing near a sign.
I went to *The Lantern* & drank near the band,
Counted his money & sipped my wine.
The barman looked at me.
'Back a winner, chum?' he said.
'I wonder how much of that you'll take home?'

'I looked up Truth in the telephone book.
Number not listed, but there on the wall
Was a scribbled name. This I took
To the girl in red who leaned in the hall.
She looked at me.
"Come upstairs, Franky," she said.
"And I'll give you a taste of home."

We rolled in the blackness. A fork, a knife.
When we were done there was scent in the air.
She closed her eyes, my five-minute wife.
I paid her nearly half of my share.
Then I looked at her.
"I want you tell me where Truth is," I said.
"It's time for her to go home."

"That's what they all say," she said.
"It forfeits delight & pleasure's misrule."
Prove me a liar. This is her bed.
Look at me lying here, in the sweat of fools.'
And then she looked at me.
'So now that you know where Truth is,' she said,
'Go out & forget her. And go home.'

Castle Labyrinth

Every kiss my father gave me
Every word that nearly saved me
Every girl that love can't quote
Every friend that called, then wrote

> *Water of the river, glass*
> *The grey fish curving above stones*
> *Walls of the castle, immersed*
> *The watcher in his psychic fast*

Every neck my hands have dreamed on
Every shoulder I've routined on
Every day a cheerful tooth
Every nice museum of youth

> *Over the drawbridge, gaieties & sighs*
> *Fluttering the breeze takes them*
> *Fish swish & are gone*
> *Pennants & perfumes & alibis*

Every well-served master, maybe
Every well-done deed, parade me
Every carefully-worded curse
Every better could do worse

> *Now it is time, messages of smoke*
> *Returning at dusk*
> *Other days are like all days today*
> *Returning at dusk*

Every chapter brooks no other
Every other needs its brother
Every truthful, lying surge
Every twice-times baffled urge

> *To turn away, perhaps, from desire*
> *The castle silent, & cold*
> *The watcher in autumn light*
> *Season of fog, & fickle fire*

Every satisfied lump that rends me
Every famished power that tends me
Every health you hope will heal
Every 'what-d'you-*really*-feel?'

Finer with time the castle / Stay
Leaves drift thru the air than yr blood
More darkness than noticed / Or breath
Realler one day than even today

Coco La Motte

The poems of La Motte, who is half African, half Belgian, strike more poses in half an hour than you or I could in a lifetime. His disbelief in popular continuance would seem to be contradicted by the fact that he is, at the time of writing, 150 years old. Come the apocalypse, his charming mixture of erudition & womanising will probably appear, like the cigarette advertisements, somewhat off the wall. [Eds. note.]

1 *My Credo*

The ticket clerk paints
nudes, vases, shipwrecks
from his *own*
imagination – VILE! –
a hobby man, a hobby life!

I have borrowed
the imagination
of the race, to paint
the SOUL of it!
that sweet research…

Within the crooked jar
of my head
vapours are mulled:
O useless alembic!
my unwashed skull

An Ad

Wanted: dark or ab-
olished tower,
suit shadow or
inconsolable, for
perusal of the infinite. Write

> *the*
> *seeker*
> *of*
> *the thing*
> *sought*

Grand Swell Central

Divested of cloak & hat
I couple with street women on lumpy beds

Breathed poetry of vulgar encounters

(then!)

The gardens at dawn

(then!)

Perfume of solitude

A Wasp

Life wakes to vicious
busy-ness. What you get
paid for over & over,
what given

falls on the
deaf, the sex-
ually paralysed, the
incompletely insane

          my message
          has been

The Telegram

Not have to accept things as are STOP

Only by anger will you make them

Not different

        Coco

2

To say something
in exactly the words
which make it true
'll make it *not*
true. A poem
is the failure of an event
which this is not

(I must for argument's sake
maintain the pose)

& a necessity
of not entirely real-
ising what
one had in mind
prevails

To be myself
I leapt from the stern of the *Orizaba*
into mythic waters,
hung as a thief,
prophesied own death on 36th birthday...

(None of these things)

3

All talk of hell
is insufferable

Is that somebody
on his knees?

I am not
on *my* knees!

...I am perfectly well aware, as one must be, that my passion for
beatitude has, at times, led me into strange places. One cannot rule
out, at any time, the possibility of an actual, shall we say, genuflection?
...made here & now upon...

anyhow not
rule out

prose?

Our language
takes nobody seriously

A cliff
is a sheer breath
of upward white

Happiness
fools no one
& then is gone

4

My agents, my pimps, my soldiers,
that proxy of my would-be valorous world,
are parked on yonder bank, like daisies.
I have kicked them before,
roused them to some indecent exertion,
whispered hot instructions
in their languid ears, but now...
Frankly, I am tempted to join them.
Being clever at the expense of God is wearisome –
God is not clever, & I
am nothing without an audience.

5   *At the Black Station*

Do you suppose I am not angry
to wait for life to happen at the *Hauptbahnhof*?
watch yellow taxis feed like gnats
on shrivelled travellers? *Wir freuen uns
dass, Sie so pünktlich gekommen sind.* BAH!

The city, the nation, existence,
is merely an assembly plan
that our inhabitants
so laughably pursue. MISERY!

I shall
abstract the directions,
the principal parts,
the glue!

6   *Cadence, A Dying Fall, You Know The Sort Of Thing*

Would what I care to write to anyone
be worth the gleaming half-truth it might avail?
Time, sardonically, to move on –
camp in a better class of hell. Break out
new morphologies of feeling, uncork
more vehement wine from the mind's gutter
& grant all ticket clerks
their journey heaven.

I was there. By the listless
motion of shadowed branches on a wall,
by a pollen haze of doubt. I seemed
a figure, eager, still
acute in my obedience to absence:

No matter that a talent angers into fragments –

I am suggestible as a half smile...

Or, when light plays between real things,
& sacred emptiness disclosed

I step there quickly, gone...

The scent, the odour, feel of smoke
drifting out of woodland from a dying fire

The Divestment

That is that
& this is this
my love, shd
that not be
enough?
Corsets, lingerie,
fine brocaded
stuff, clips &
fasteners touch
you, garments
of promise ad-
vertise you,
little straps, sheer
gloves, a feather
belt of swan's
net, slightly
electrical mesh.
Why is it
still
not quite enough
to fumble
at this satin
reticle, free-
ing off
the lovecatch I
have so in-
delicately
un-
hook't...?

Geography

when

I felt the heavy thrust
of yr body rising to meet mine

I felt

the heavy thrust
of yr body rising to meet mine when

the heavy thrust

of yr
body rising to meet mine when I felt

of yr body

rising to meet mine
when I felt the heavy thrust

rising

to meet mine when I felt the
heavy thrust of yr body

to meet mine

the map had me
& my boat ran aground

dragging my crew of senses
the boat had me

& my map ran aground

*   *   *

gently
as tho sleep

& doubt
were imminent

I was berthed
& swung there

the current
had undone me

(of what
will undo me

I have
the master-plan)

Teatro Greco, Taormina

Empedocles went up Etna
looking for Truth
& fell in.

It looks peaceful now. A
clear March day, framed
                              between the pillars,
few
tourists except
for you & me, until

a crowd of Italian infants,
very grown-up South
European infants,
traipse across the stage:

'Ello! 'Ow are you? E?

I scowl

      The stone seating arrangements

         Yes

      This bit is Roman
      That Greek . This
      was knocked down

I can imagine the gladiator's role

Sweating here
while the citizens find their places

      Lions

        My oiled body

> The captain of the animals
>   is grinning at me un-
> compassionately

A great cry goes up

& I walk out to face
a draggle of gaily-coloured kids
eager
to practise their English

'Ello! All right, mister?

All right

You like Liverpool? Rangers?

I like . I like

E, mister? She lady yr wife?

But not really imagine
how children's voices
might suddenly

from brute thrust of blind muzzle,
                bleed
like failing light
        into the ground, that
chirp of interest
flooding out to silence, all
to be brushed away soon by horses, pulling
a wooden harrow across the sand

Next question?

Balance : Act

Often the edge
is like a disaster; walking
                         up
yr knifeline, the rain
scratches & pricks at
                    thought

You have been with me now
for longer
than any catastrophe. My
                      nerve
twitches & I
believe the right things
                   never
happen. Still

there is always next time.
We shall lie
side by side in the darkness.
Yr breath is like milk

The shadows of yr body
paralyse the rain

Poem Ending with a Title by Benjamin Péret

Without people there would be no journeys,
And without journeys there would be no dreams,
Without dreaming there would be no poems,
Without poems...*this rhetoric's a scream*...

What we have here is the natural inclination
Of the grammar to run away with the bone

And the mood of the poet
Contemplating the abrupt departure, versification...

He'd prefer right now to be lewd
With the barmaid Sonya. *Write me a sonnet, love.*

Life becoming like, & thus explicable...
Move like that.

Words & embraces, sweetie...shouldn't they be inextricable?
Remove yr hat.

Spottiswoad

Interests himself in gurgles
of all types, especially
the prolonged gargle, or
any ineffable glug.

He has an ear too for
the clang. An erotic clang
such as Sunday morning
markedly excites him.

When out walking with
Spottiswoad, he will
strike the daylight, ex-
claiming: 'Can't you hear it ping!'

A remarkable observer, Spot-
tiswoad spots
every fleck, twinkle & speck.
How hectically he articulates

a passion for pools!
He is urgent about lulls.
A hiatus will displace him.
He loves larking, lacunae & labyrinths.

I spoke to Spottiswoad
most severely.
I said: 'Spottiswoad!
You are an instrument of perturbation!'

He flinched at my remonstration.
'I adore the maleficence
of carping,' he said.
'Pouting simply enthralls me!'

Spottiswoad is remarkable.
He collects dead echoes,
also the dust from sneezes
& the dew from pain.

In his library
the bones of the past
rebelliously excogitate
upon their shelves.

He has labelled them all:
'A Throb' 'A Remorse' 'An Intimation'.
'Like little pebbles,' says Spottiswoad,
'So discrete, intact, yet disobedient!'

His *bibliothèque* is a bowl
of extraordinary pretensions:
It lurches with unseemliness.
It vibrates with virulence.

There, a bygone phallic fury
bleeds & whole millenia
tumultuously mutiny –
blindedly, gropingly, gasping for air!

Heavy Goods

I see, generally speaking,
that what we are doing

is wrong. I see it
quite clearly, like a lorry,

a green lorry
delivering Spanish fruit

from Barcelona to Stockholm.
It goes along the road.

It is difficult, of course,
to say precisely

what one can do
about this lorry. The solution

wavers, like an interesting
building, hidden by houses,

one cannot entirely
get into view – although

quite sharp in bits.
Furthermore

it is clear that our
ideas of what is right,

notions of love, marriage,
family & profit,

are, in themselves,
not unlike the whale: that is to say

the laborious mammoth
we slay for catfood.

Let us console ourselves
with the thought

that some people
are saving it. For the whale

is dying out. Its
reluctance to transmit

electronic messages
makes it redundant.

What will the sea be like
if the door is left open

& all the fish swim out?
I imagine it

rather like Neptune,
hunched & disconsolate,

where the plug, unstoppered,
still gurgles faintly:

his feet
in the mud.

It is also quite clear to me
that faced with difficulty

a man should be
an orange. Of Spanish origin

or Swedish destination
is immaterial. He will

require a red string bag
in which to contain himself,

jostling agreeably with
other oranges. He will

come to know roundness,
sameness & hardness,

&, not to mince matters,
will have to stay there.

Travel is not important,
as an orange cannot see

where it is going – will not
regret Barcelona or deplore Stockholm.

One further thing: it is
characteristic of oranges that they

will be cut open & squeezed.
I cannot see this as wrong.

There should be nothing left in you
when you are finished. Also,

the lorry – & I see this
quite clearly now –

is only glimpsed *en route*
so to speak. For it never arrives.

Derbyshire Grotto

Rivers have made me weep
& engines blinded; a postcard
from the kiosk shows the falls.
Why do I not so, with Jenny &
George, walk to the grotto
turnstile, click my money to
the vulgar boatman, let myself
upon the dark tide squeal
pinching her bottom? Reasons?

Ah well, when the snow comes,
think. My shadow will still
be here, in a kind of prayer.
Silence in the car-park, no ticket issued
for my pew. How barren the
landscape without chatter! How
the whiteness drifts over everything,
pinching my mind with its
ah! – sibilance! – cold at the groin, in
the palm of the hand, at heart.

No, no. I am spoken for. We
breakfasted late. I breathe the
air. No, no. I am committed,
merely I wait. The roads
& weather brought me here. There is
no excuse. We travel alone.
Last night she shook in the cataclysm
of sexual despair, her loins
like razors. As for myself? I am
modest, deprecate the soft asylum
– I await the real lunatic!

Dawn Beach

From here to the turn of the century
is hardly a mile

as the bat flies, zig-zag, thru pitch
nothingness.

They seem so pleased with themselves over there.
It must be better than it is now. Or was:

cities fouled, mud & dullness
kicking their heels round the outskirts,

poor numbskulls throttled for a penny,
waifs abused, mis-used...

Now we have brilliant golf-balls
of lucid & sinister harmony

& later a curious blackness
so near you can reach out & touch it.

It will be hot, like an animal that
has been sleeping on the refrigerator,

or an arm that twists out of darkness
around you, deliberate with desire.

Luckily, trains run out to the edges of the city,
taking me with them.

Nothing has changed much here. Chickens scratch.
Sprouts flower. A few sheds tumble quietly.

From here to the future
is but a few clods of earth.

And beyond that
is the pallor of wasteland in the early dawn.

Huge pylons tramp the cow-flecked grass.
Some trees echo of forests. History is flat.

And across it, vibrating & buzzing,
hurtle the illuminated trucks, carrying wealth.

Consignments of money pass by on the high road
above our stooped backs, where we inspect for worms –

the reassuring sight of worms,
slithering, concertina-ing.

I believe I should engage my neighbour in conversation,
but he has walked some distance off, absorbed.

He is glancing a spade at the Metazoic,
sheer & clean, the downward layers of the future.

How does it look to him? Or to me, for that matter?
What one can immediately comprehend, I mean?

Sounds of a radio come from the lighted window
of his caravan. Frying smells in the morning air.

My neighbour's wife. Her breasts. Her warm tongue.
I am lapped on an invisible shore,

something restless, cast up, willing to be sucked back,
willing to go forward, struggling against the idea of it.

It is in that moment I know she is God.
She does not even bother to undress properly.

God remains cloaked for want of time, as we know.
And it is not long from here to there.

What shall we say? The city blazes to my right.
She is at my elbow.

When I come finally to the door, & look out
I see the twenty-first century as clearly as a cat.

It is moving along the wall, slinking, & stops.
It faces me, its pre-historic head, its green eyes:

A look of such incomprehensible significance
I can only nod, half-bemusedly. And it vanishes.

A god too, perhaps? I hear her behind me, rustling.
The stroke of nyloned legs. The voice of invitation: 'Come.'

And the rule of sunlight pitches up above the skyline
like the beginning of some new & terrible game.

Sunday

A virgin lifts the piano lid
upstairs & starts the metronome.
Unbawdy melodies wing forth,
heartfelt as a gramophone!

Below, he's feeling up his soul,
& reading thru the weekend gloom.
The papers make a devastating
leaflet crater of the room.

Come back, my lover, come! Jesus Christ!
This was a day for malign reflection,
& now a nympholeptic tune
has given him a slow erection!

Result? He suddenly feels mad,
grabs the wife, stops her mouth & brings
her to her knees. In her ear
he whispers all these awful things:

> *Too much & too important is my heart.*
> *You, you're only human, flesh & spittle.*
> *So don't take it too hard will you,*
> *if I should hurt you just a little!*

The Ideology

Germaine Greer has a thing
      about the consumerist couple
prolonging active orgasm
    'die Pflicht der Freude'

                you might say, &
                therefore
                French knickers in grey
                champagne silk
                and all
                the paraphernalia

necessary for
'man's inordinately long life'.

I think of this
as we enter *Hennes & Mauritz*
                to purchase
the sd garment
& I walk from the
                trying-on room
                back
to the rail
for a smaller size

                'man's inordinately
                long
                journey across
                the lingerie department'

holding
that small thing
made in
Shanghai

                to the imperial ﹨
                delight of
                severed fingertips...

Later, in bed, I pull
out the three studs
at the crotch, like water

                 you are, pleased,
                 running thru my palm
                 as we dawdle out
                 high above the bar *'Zum Ambrosius:*
                 Ein Begriff in Berlin'
                 toward pleasure...

Ah, society's
inordinately long
sub-fertile

                 wandering
                 in sweet sateen...

Until at 3 a.m.
we hear the cops
placate a fracas
in the joint

Seven Ways of Looking at a Frog

1

Today's lecture
is common
or garden
or frog.

Now, the frog is an amphibian.
He cannot actually fly.

He crosses countless wet roads
to reach his beloveds.
He is a jamjar of aspirations.

No extra-terrestrial beings
have quite his
rasp of fact.
Remember:
you only exist if
he thinks of you

So:

(If you should hear
a noise in the moonlight

it is probably a frog
sawing the planet in half.)

2 *A Dance*

You frog to the left,
you frog to the right.

       You frog all around you.

Then you frog it all night.

3

Frog.

Green & waterloving frog.

Very biologically old frog.

Frog of metamorphoses.
Frog that I love to catch
& put down my daughter's shirt.

Or, even better,
down the shirt of my neighbour's plump wife.

Frog!

What are you doing down there?

4

Woman
is desirable.

Woman plus frog,
more so.

5

If you let a frog go
it just keeps on hopping
till it reaches the garden fence
& then keeps on hopping
till it reaches somewhere else
& then just bloody well keeps on hopping
till it comes back looking surprised.

6

A frog has relations.
There's Peter Frog, Helen Frog,
Archibald Frog & Melpomene Frog.
They do not live far away.
They are always coming round for Sunday Lunch.
One frog would like to abandon his lilypad
& head for the hills with Melpomene.
Not nice & frog-like behaviour at all, this,
introducing a tapioca-like substance into the equation.
(It resembles jelly, but passes for life.)

Tadpole mathematics, dear boy.
The whistling stars. This froggy horoscope.

Infinity grows larger
with every hop of hope.

7

They are wailing
in bogs of harmony,

delicious, Irish,
revolutionary tunes.

Their miseries achieve
symphonic heights

then stop.

Would the time, now,
just before they stopped

be more perfect than
the time just after they stopped?

Or might it be that
thru inattention

to the exact moment of ceasing
you could have missed

the most perfectly frog-like moment
of all?

Coda for Frog & Angelic Choir

When a frog dies
it goes to heaven
with its hands in its pockets.

It leans against a lamp post.
It tips its hat to Beatrice,
                    to Miranda.
It proposes easy ways of making money.

The frog is interviewed
by the people in charge.
This has just got to stop, you understand.

The frog shrugs.
It is his nature.
I was thinking of moving out anyway,
he says

& gives a mighty spring.

Today, of All Days

I hung myself up into the new morning
& my long legs dangled down.
Between them, luxuriously free,
a clothes peg danced upon the line.
I washed myself up
& cleared away the wishes.
The milk & sugar world beyond the window
lay starving in
a ghostly breakfast bowl of snow.

I lit the radio & boiled myself
a thought. Three minutes. The place
required careful reading &
re-reading. Walls are a fiction
to interpret all right. The transition from
one door to the next
demanded fixing. The image of the floor
was good, good, good...
I was standing on it.

Back into bed was best,
but found myself in the bath.
The sheets gurgled out. I was left
to dry. Toenails! They needed
editing. Was my sallow nakedness
not in quite good taste just here,
or should it stand there?
Ah! I should like to take hold of my darling,
but she is letting in the cold.

So many things to do.
Have to keep jumping up to close her.
Get the coal from the imagination.
Phone reality about the roof.
Dream-bills to be paid. Future to be repaired.
I poured myself a cup of her body
& folded to the puzzle page. One across:
'The endless brightness of love
shouldn't be left burning all night.'

What kind of anagram was that?
The day was beginning to look
as if someone had lost it.
Headlines, a difficult believableness.
On my domestic staff were one or two
I could wolfishly violate.
If the mirror wouldn't mend its ways
I'd have to let it go. Or worse.
Either way, something would happen. It did.

Osgood

Osgood! Are these neatly-folded
garments yrs? Why, the edge of this
high building is a precipice! Look
how the gulls flock & swarm!
Is this emphasis something
you have left behind, something
we should all take hold of, or is it,
well is it just...the usual?
Osgood! Why fly naked? I would have
loaned you my cloak, if I had known!

Excuse me, it is Mr Osgood, isn't it?
I was his friend, that is
to say we were *amitié* personified, if
sharing flats, beer-money, women, taxis,
old cars, shirts, razor-blades,
bedclothes, cigarettes, ideas about life,
Sunday newspapers, horror of the future
is friendship. Is it? I thought it was,
then. But of course I'm older now.
How old would you say I was? Just guess.

It's astonishing, it really is.
You're as perfectly made as the weather.
Yr predictions always come true with time.
(Ha ha. So does time, I know.)
To see you approaching one feels
the overruled sensation of the blind.
Why, Osgood, you are magniloquent!
Yr purposeful silence would thrill a hush.
The nerves of air vibrate when you're around
& the world looks up, stops, & starts again.

O Osgood, do this, will you? And that?
Do it at once, Osgood. You're a good chap.
Osgood, I have news for you. You've
heard of Osgood? Excellent fellow. Time he
received his due. Osgood,
the contribution you've been making fills us all.

I have to give way, Osgood. The better man.
Why don't you...? Osgood?
I seem to find you looking like that
at high buildings. Disturbance of clouds.

Dear Peter, it is so long
since I heard from you. I am well.
Now I live in Australia, as you will see
from the stamp. I am married & we have
three children & a nice ark nearby
just in case. You can run here, along
the edge of white, breathing Southern air,
the absence of a lot of things.
One day perhaps you will write, please,
& say what you are doing. All my.

Did you hear about Osgood? He jumped!
Jumped? Osgood? But he had to live for
everything. There was nothing he couldn't!
Every time he, everyone was simply.
Only yesterday it came to my mind.
But when you think that for nearly ten years.
Ten years! Of course, he was always.
Perhaps it was inevitable if you think.
Yes. And you know he was always.

True.

Snowdancing

We danced in the snow.

But this is not true.

All day, climbing,
we became fiends of purpose.
Faces I had never seen before
became familiar as light.
Then it grew dark.

There was a tiny prickling
of coloured bulbs, dripping
radiance as from a melting
icicle, rainbow-like.
The band airily played a vehicle.
Rumbas went in & out
thru singing doors, like waiters.
They danced in the snow.

Ah, but they did not.

It was so cold & pure outside.
We whirled away
into the musical darkness.

Without regret or tenderness,
they came up to you & touched you.
They were like curious wolves.
It hardly mattered
that their embraces were so
extraordinary, without
feeling, or with some kind of
snow. Perhaps you were touched
only to be gone again.
Perhaps, penetrated, you
were released like ice.
And the stars were full of quietness.

Hearts had been happily happening.
One after another they joined
                              in a long line,
stretching from the doorway outwards,
holding hands to the edge
of the precipice (lest one
fall over in the dark),
& the furthest out leaned over, calling:

'There they are!
Dancing in the snow!'

Ah, but they were not.

Elegy

Inside the sadness of a man
who has chopped down his last tree
there is an empty place
where the shade fell, & the chairs
& the table, & the missing people
were cool, out of the sunlight.

Curiously, the man is not sad.
He has concentrated upon two main things:
Upon going further. And going wider.
These occupy him like a pair of gloves.
His wife meanwhile
takes care of the darkness. The visitors listen.

Only those of us who know
what the man was, or could have been,
drink of that sadness in small cups,
seated behind a window. We would like to go.
It is as if they were not our trees, after all.
It is as if we had not been here, even tho we had.

Eskimo

Fat to fat, fur to fur, squashed nose to lip,
O for the igloo of that cold contentment!

The youth dreamed of it. He was like a garment
Found on a rag-pile, ripped –
No skin within that wind-pocked coat
No palms to warm the pocket's hollow
No fingers groping from the cuffs, no throat
Beating with blood against a filthy collar,
Trousers hoisted on a skinny column,
Air, they hung in knives about his shanks,
Codpiece holding someone else's cod, mmm
Yr jacksex kind a world of flesh outflanks:

Arms above his head, crouched low,
A cornerless person, waiting for snow.

Desire

is shaved tight, ample in hair & flesh,
           cunning in loose corners
is mule-stubborn at sheer buildings,
           iconoclastic in warm white sheets
is eager to interview the woman between
           spaces of roof & sky
is next, always next, always arriving, never gone, never
           punctual, hopeful, so hopeful...

Desire

changes the way you walk, slips under the paving stones,
           under an undone belt of the passer-by
gets into yr eyes like sleep or glaucoma, fumbles with
           the way things look
acts in no precise way, no predestinations, no ambitions,
           no strategies...all these
fills the sufferer with burning benevolence, all kinds of
           faithful lies, a glowing grail of trash

Desire

places her before the gorilla-god, his humped & submissive
           stance
breathes in the flesh of discarded clothing, respiration of
           shadows, endings, beginnings...
makes turn the lovely head, the straight back, the rosy
           mould of spine & skin
tenders the ghost of a temple embrace, in the vale
           of her arms, the vault of complicity...

Desire

is a secret kept from facts, endlessly concluded, mingling
           with trees & paths
is a picture burned against laughter, freezing against
           talk, silent against belief
when the time comes, as it always does
is freedom's secret, the journey undertaken beyond hope or grasp
           of time

Desire

    squats on its raft, yr pathetic flag & tattered torso
         glimpsed on the navigable eye
    soars toward the readymade instant, again & again
         hurls itself into the unknown frame
    repudiates & clutches, rescues & drowns, cries out & is
         grateful, for only (finally)
    overboard, becomes what the sacred becomes

Desire

    will always be betrayed
    the cave painting at Lascaux
    is the bull, the hull of the bull in the hall of the marvellous
    time in its original colour, not
    the dark wall worked by torchlight, but the image
    of vanished itself in the trembling, where only
    the breathing of absence brings air to yr throat,
    the forgotten, where close
    is to choke
    for

Desire

    accepts no form other than the form of first contact

    * * *

    does not speak, there is no creed, nakedness the text, a
         slow, sinew-rounding gospel of the silence

    * * *

    is without intellect, or cognition, lean then against her

    * * *

    resists the fantastic organisation it absurdifies, a
         hierarchy of becoming

    Rests within itself & struggles to emerge
    Beyond the appraisal of the present circumstances, vomits

Excoriates what is spoken of, desires simply
Races back to itself to go beyond, desires

For we have spoken of something
That has no name

Not to name it, but to speak of it
Not to identify it, for this is possible

No tradition after all :

The polished ploughshare catching the sun
The dull earth, the following tread,
And the rooks, mad biological confusions...

Devils, devils in black coats swarming up the ladder, not
        to be ignored

In Wonderland

The naked were done with their nakedness
Our maids reversed themselves
We viewed things differently & grew smaller
Then we grew enormous & cd not get thru the door
'Who are you?' sd the caterpillar, disgruntled
It was not a philosophical question

'I know what I did this morning, sir, but that
Was somebody else. There were, I recall
A lot of disappearing men in top hats.'
'Mmm,' sd the caterpillar, 'so they *were* imported mushrooms…
And when the queen says, *"Off with their heads…!"*
I suppose you appreciate the sexual significance of that?'

'O, the artillery!' breathed Alice. 'Of course!'

Maids, babies, pigs… all inverted slowly out of joy

A Corner of the Garden

Things of beauty, not much
joy forever,
                    tyres & a steel pole,
a flapping sheet
                    of dirty polythene,
logs stacked anyhow

the idle, incurious labour
of one who
                    has not long to live

& daffodils
                    dashed
from early-morning
                    hose-water
striving
to recover the flesh

                    of 10,000 limbs

I wish
I were a fat
dirty white & ginger Jack
pussycat

                    prowling...

or a bicycle
leaned against the drainpipe
in the sun

                    I wish

                              upright behind the shed
                              I had been that
                              particular
                                        green rake
                              for at least 20 years / no one

                              has raked with

                    to be the owner
                    of this disconsolate corner
                    of time

to step from the crumbling house
two-cornered white sleeping-cap on,
in a stinky housecoat,
with roubles in my ears,
breathing garlic, morning beer

                    & a pickled egg

               plucking my daffodils
               my pretties / one by one

& take you inside
yr prickly stamens, ye saffron
                              dust,
yr slenderness, stem-like, reaching
the greasy raft of my pillow
extending thy long body
where the stains of sleep / tears
                              & misadventure
offer their cunning protections

                    have you embrace me thus
                    thy whole length touched
                    in every inch to mine

A Walk

Thoughts of you
            drive
me along, the wind
               drives
back
        I picture you
        lace-gartered in black
        high-cupped breasts
        a tanga, yr white hips
              fleecy & smooth
        against material

           Two
           silent women
                  on bicycles
           creak by

Is the landscape really so flat
where yr body
under the curve of my walk

takes me, re-
tracing the touch of touch?

        Between
        the opening
        of two mind-ricks

                you pose against a white wall
                for my regard's
                ultimate snapshot, yr

willingness, is it, to
enact?

                Do it.

        And the image moves...

I have been pushing on,
a forgetful shadow,
into the occasional emptiness

    when a house

        in sudden light

            stops me.

Pink wall
Quietness
The dog
raises its head...
An open door

I'm looking at you

Sunlight across the threshold, that
darkness inside

        What would it
        be like, the
        view from yr
        nakedness?

   the s   from the pearl
     l   roundness
      o   of yr shoulder
       p
        e

        of yr body

        that
        blinding
        narrowness

                       to the still
                       but definitely
                       moving land
                       beyond?

Rolling Road

I was muddy & I was ditch.
The farmers received a premium for this disorder.

There was money for brambles, rusting barbed wire,
old implements buried in dock leaves

to snag yr foot, snap off yr ankle, bring you down...
There was a subsidy for pollution by gas.

It sneezed all over the landscape
& we staggered as the farmers smiled

to see their cripple cash crop
paper the horizon, like dancingmen.

But there were no farmers. There was just
the smile that intensively laboured to produce

further smiles. And all the smiles contained
no landscapes of any sort that cd be recognised.

And no amelioration of this, except
the iron hand of a would-be seducer, the hook

under a maiden's skirt, & she terrified, not
moving as the silky steel climbed a thigh.

And no, there was no hook, but the eyes
of a girl I undistractedly loved

as I wandered thru ruts & bogwater,
thru sighs of sucking ground, like

the lungs of my dying playfellows,
thru slowly collapsing barns of desire

in which only the smell of seed cd be ascertained.
I looked up & saw the sky...

Such a breathlessly unintelligent act, to
perceive the corroded tin, fallen open to starlings.

Yet there was no maiden. No barn.
Imagine, tho, its structure had been her body,

its twisted pillars her legs,
its great, airy, colander-like vacancy

a half-collapsed place in which I cd saunter,
its missing roof her trepanned head…

I wd have been able to hear
the restlessness of bulls & pigs moving

in the dark stall of their fidelity,
& breathe her snide female openness.

And none of it was
possible, myself being

upon a lane that led nowhere, if it led round.
I was the circumperambulant gesture of my time

at which all laughed dutifully. They had
nothing else to do. And I walked.

I led my gesture up hill & down dale.
I doublewent myself. A speck on the road.

And slowly the ghost-crop of the farmers
pushed thru the weeds on all sides

& ripped open my orientation with a fine green carpet
that stretched far in all directions. And I

called it a harvest. Did I plant it?
I looked at it with stupefaction & nodded my head.

Yes.
The transparent ditch.

Dance

Buckwheat lay yr darning down
And come with me to revel town.
I want to play, I want to sing,
With you, I want everything.

The city bars are red. Are blue.
Crowds are black. The night is rue.
Lamplight throws a gleaming dart
Along the shadows of the heart.

I want to drink, I want to dance,
I want the city's neon avalanche
To fall on me & bury me
Beneath the tribes of revelry.

Do not be sad with silent dreams,
Each day will fade, & so will dreams.
Buckwheat take yr cold cloak off
And come with me to Maximov's.

I need when all the antic's gone
To sleep with you in silent song,
And hold yr warm-sweat body close,
Let dreams turn into empty ghosts.

Dance with me, my Buckwheat, dear,
Along the pavement, down the year
Of this one-coloured life we're sold
Until we drunkenly grow old.

Above all else I wish to do
Is wake each morning next to you,
And wake, remembering, to light,
The things we really did last night.

O Buckwheat lay yr darning down.
Come with me to revel town.
With you I want to play & sing.
Do now, the next, the future thing.

Tending Grill

Žar is the word
            for the ash
to cook with

a little hard wood, *bagrem*,
blazed to a scrupulous tilth
               of fire
& the mesh across it

I sit here
sipping *rakija*
      & watch
the burning crop
whiten & dislocate
          into fact

in the dust
a segment of the wood
             remains
        like some
infernal crocodile, half-
           submerged
in flame

it is decomposing, be-
coming pale powder
         hotter
than brand
      or iron
against my face
to testify:

        the meat is good

        la chair est triste

        but not

        alas

Podrum na Selo

It's like coming home

The yeast-smell
                of the wine-cellar...

These gallons casked
in gloom /
            so many
                        yellow
journeys to
misremembering . One

                year's

                        crop:

                                Kevedinka
                                Ezerjo
                                Rizling

                the roll-call
                of grapes...

He un-bungs a
single barrel

                the
                    brown
                rubber
                        tube
                snakes
                    in

&
  he
      sucks
&
  the

vat pukes
in golden
  gouts

     sluicing a
     milk-churn . Afterwards
     the air burnt off
        a sulphur flare
     inserted rips out
     oxygen then
     the stopper's rammed in

     500 litres
     700 litres
     400 litres

shadow back into
the cobwebbed room 'a science'

you would say, as

he measures
ladles
pours

     'of amnesia
     perhaps...'

this low-slung, sideways-tipping cottage
its curling roof of tiles
poplar trees, leafless in March
bare alleys of the vineyard, pruned

    old men
    moving across
    the hard ground...

     You have the urge, I know
     to leave this place,
        to

scatter

    night

        with selves

    Be distances . Seek
    other pleasures . Drink
    the canary roar
    in yr ear

        The universe
        is broached with yr forgetfulness . It
        flows a-
        cross the ragged sill of stars, en-
        gulfing
        walls of white-washed wattle
        propped
        by spider scaffolding . It
        stains
        earth's floor, seeps in . A

    smile . An

irony

of reeking body-smell
of pale brow above the hatline
of greedy & grosstender hands
of / seriousness, planetmade . Well,

        let him reckon it out then :

        this year's crop
        hailstorms in April
        early frost / sunshine / how

        much it will cost you
        this time

        exactly

The Killer of Mulfatty

Mulfatty's killer
is waiting in raincoat
his gun in his hand
& his eyes on the end.
He's gripped by a memory.
What did he do there? Who
did he kill? There, by
the corner of street-lamp
& wall? Out of the many
he killed Mulfatty. Many
of all of us might do the same.
He was paid with her body –
a night of delirium. He knew
it was useless, he won't take the blame.
Death was agreed on.
He was the agent.
Look at him, wordless. You are his name.

The police are out hunting
with yatta-ta-ta guns. Their
violence deafens, their nostrils flare.
His picture's on television
now, where we're eating
tuna-fish sandwiches, too doped
to care. O it is awful.
What is he called?
Down come the snowflakes, down
comes the dark, the failure
of all of you, each in his past.
He'll make a run for it.
It's no good. It's thumbsdown,
throw fate a bone. He looks at
his timepiece of Japanese chrome,
tugs at his braces, flexes
his calves. His underthings, ripped, have
the grace of disgrace. Will death
find him suitable, or do things
by halves? A megaphone blares.
Fraud-lamps are on him.
He's alone with yr stares.

We watch on our smallscreens,
mouths mewed with food.
Can you imagine him? Sprawled
on a bed with him? Sharing
a sweet? Our killer is skinny,
tattoos on his arm.
We should be frightened
by what he may harm. Watching,
we watch him, our jaws nearly
stopped. He seizes
a schoolgirl & walks into sight:
'Kill me, she dies,' he shouts,
wondering: 'Where run to?'
There's only a wall, &
the bricks of the light.

An agon of bullets
removes him to Heaven. We
take out our guns &
get ready to shoot. Yes
he is saved, it is our turn
to play. We're flattened to walls,
listening to steps. Our mouths
full of sandwich, we ponder
the worth of it, killing Mulfatty
has won no applause.
He was bushy with prizes,
oiled with fame. The words
of his deeds were like weeds
in a garden. We loved her,
we killed him:
we'd a world to betray.
I see ourselves running
then fall very slow.

For the ache of her glamour,
the click of our pleasure,
we slew poor Mulfatty:
it's our turn to go.
The girl dies. The killer dies.
He writes with a finger
in boot-trampled snow.

Don't read this. Pass by me.
This is not yet
the end of the show.

A Moment of Truth in 'Le Bar du Château'

Canals ruminate on spoiled air,
gluttonous and placid. I love
ships, dung and water; credulous
emotions sparking on rubbish.

The trees are mute, the blowsy
water glooms. Along the path: 'Le Bar
du Château' and a slattern griping
from the doorway into deadening afternoon.

'Bonjour!' 'Bonjour!' Thank God it's empty.
Tables and pinball and the barman, his
grotesquely fleshy arms upon the counter,
anchoring the Sunday Paper with tattoos.

Headlines: *'J'adore Jésus Christ!'*
'La Sainte Vièrge est ma Copine'. In turbid
eyes his soul skulks like a pike, toils
to raise salvation in a glass of *Meuse*.

The paint drips. Plastic table-cloths
urge retreat. The slut enfeebles me;
I'm devoured with belief, necessity of dirt,
the callous come-on, the easy perfumed breath.

Rain rots through leafless branches.
Sucking air the ruined water swells
to marvellous dimensions, pouring through
the hull, clutching the keel, gulping

through the portholes: all is distended
in this vile bladder. I am in love
helplessly. Chairs, tables, beerglasses,
I kiss you all, as tears stain my cheeks.

Muse

Well, & if the goddess came stumbling in
Kicked over the empties, joined me on the mattress
I know there'd be someone upstairs screaming
'Can't you control that girl of yrs?'
But she'd make no noise. She'd be the soul,
                            the heart of silence

So I lie here on this bed
Blessed with boredom, the energy of nothingness
And thrill to her non-existent kiss
I know she's waiting for me on a street corner
Hiking her skirt, smoking a cigarette...

And I know it's too cold out there. And foggy
And I'm too lazy to put on my coat & go
And she'll be waiting anyhow, sometime, somewhere
Like Truth in a Waiting Room, patient, on a chair...

My Little Waggonette

Going for a ride recently
I was thinking of people, & how chilling
It is to experience correctly
The Perspicuity of Fools

I had a late romance of intelligence
Roads were the trees of her arms
An adored bumpiness. She called
My destiny a pothole. She murmured:

'The great thing about disasters
Happening to other people
Is also true of crucifixions
They become cathedrals, later...'

In those over-large buildings
Everyone was applauding the enemy
I opened the door, & the candles blew out
By the Grace of God she was swept against me

I was shaken to pieces on ruts
Sacred places had wide enough doors
To swallow me, wagon & all
A covered park of nails & jeers

We plodded thru hanging orchards
Past decrepit byre & pen
Turned in at the daisy yard
A landscape splattered with dung

Up in the hayloft with a girl
The landlord picked seeds from her mouth
If I were tender & had no form
I'd write like the river of youth

A crazy estate, this body
Deep sunken lanes thru dreams
Carpentry not humanity
Makes a roof of my spine...See

How I just go on fretting
At the support structure holds it up
Her horizon is my exit
Her soul is always asleep

She's the one my resolve
Wanted least to feel awkward about
I take her from my pocket, make
This cupped-hand gesture to the Lord of Doubt

Final

Each train of broken thought

           stranger & pilgrim

    so we fail
    to arrive, as
    on the white steamship
    read the lettering,

             clear-

ly it says:

        MIDNIGHT LINE

a few sentences
a few hopes
the smell of food

& the gabble of
exited passengers